PRIZE
Awarded to

THOMAS SZTEJER

for

EFFORT PRIZE - FORM 2

Date   JULY 1988

PHILIP & TACEY LTD Andover Hants   Ref. 046-003-000

Junior naturalist

IN THE COUNTRY

WRITTEN BY
KEN HOY

ILLUSTRATED BY
ADRIAN RIGBY

DESIGNED BY
GRAHAM BROWN

WARD LOCK

First Published in Great Britain by
Ward Lock Limited, 82 Gower Street,
London WC1E 6EQ. 1985

© Brown Wells and Jacobs Limited, London. 1985

Written by Ken Hoy
Illustrations by Adrian Rigby
Designed by Graham Brown
Typesetting by Words & Pictures Limited
Colour Originated by RCS Graphics Limited
Printed and Bound by Henri Proost & CIE PVBA.

British Library Cataloguing in Publication Data

Hoy, Ken
    Junior naturalist in the country.
    1. Natural history—Great Britain—Juvenile
    literature
    I. Title   II. Rigby, Adrian
    574.941   QH137

ISBN 0-7063-6376-0

CONTENTS

COUNTRYSIDE BEGINS

Long before history, men and women lived by hunting, fishing and gathering wild foods. This was happening in Britain after the great sheets of ice melted more than 10,000 years ago. Another 4,000 years went by before the first signs appear of another way of getting food.

About 6,000 years ago we are told by archaeologists there began to be changes. By examining layers of mud and peat (decayed vegetation) with a microscope it is possible to find grains of pollen. In the peat that was made about 6,000 years ago the amounts of pollen from trees began to decrease and the pollens from grasses and many of the field plants we call "weeds", like Ribwort Plantain suddenly increased very markedly. However the pollens of Birch, Hazel and Alder trees increased among the tree pollens.

We believe that these changes indicate that men were clearing the thick woodlands and were growing crops for two or three years before moving to new areas. Trees and scrub would then regrow and the first trees to recolonise would certainly be the quick growing birch trees.

These clearings in the woods were the first fields.

Experts now believe that as long as 5,000 years ago many of our river valleys and most of the hills and upland moors were probably clear of trees and supporting farms that grazed animals and grew crops.

It is possible that by 3,000 years ago as much of the country was farmed as we have being worked today by farmers.

Often the very early farmers were of two kinds, as the story of Cain and Abel makes clear, those who grazed animals – sheep, goats, cattle and horses – and those who grew crops. This involved a completely different way of life. The grazing or pastoral people needed to move with their animals to wherever they could graze and these people therefore were nomadic. Farmers growing crops had to live in one place at least for a growing season until they could harvest the crop. In river valleys where the soil was very fertile or where flooding renewed the fertility they were able to settle more permanently.

Roman writers reported that British farmers spread chalk on their fields on a widespread scale to improve its growing capacity. Later, in the Middle Ages, crop rotation was practiced, that is growing different crops each year on the same field and then "resting" this land for a year by leaving it "fallow". This and the cattle enriching the fields with their dung enabled settled farming to occur.

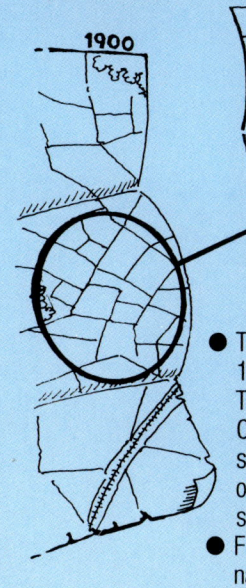

YOUR COUNTRYSIDE

What kind of countryside is near your home? Are there fields? Where are the nearest fields?

● What are the fields used for? Growing crops? Grazing animals?

● How are they divided? By hedges, fences of wood or wire, stone walls, banks or ridges, ditches, dykes or open drains?

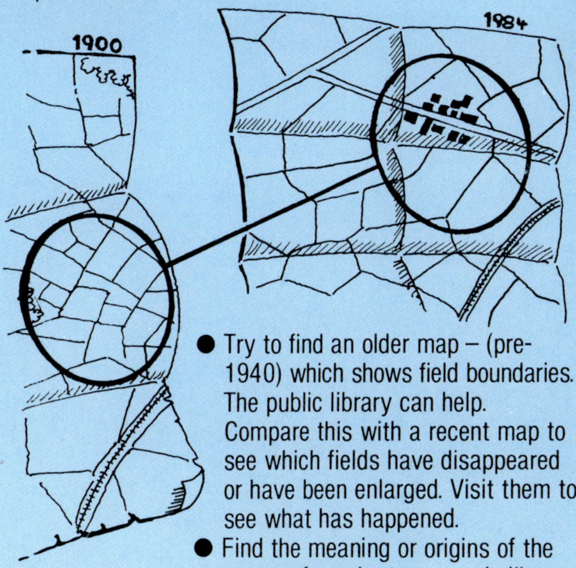

1900

1984

● Try to find an older map – (pre-1940) which shows field boundaries. The public library can help. Compare this with a recent map to see which fields have disappeared or have been enlarged. Visit them to see what has happened.

● Find the meaning or origins of the names of nearby towns and villages. A book of 'place-names' in the library will help you.

TODAY'S COUNTRYSIDE

Bales of hay from a hill-farm

For hundreds of years, until the middle of the present century, most farmers grew crops and reared animals on their land. These are called "mixed farms".

Modern farms have become more specialised and operate on a larger scale. Consequently many changes have taken place. However to some extent the type of soil and whether the farmland is on a hillside or in a valley still affects what it can or cannot be used for.

There are upland farms containing mostly rough grazing where, only some breeds of sheep and one or two types of cattle can flourish in the harsh conditions, and summers are too short for crops to grow. At the other extreme there are rich river valleys where the best use of the soil is to grow many quick crops on an intensive scale; this is sometimes called 'market gardening'. Vegetables, fruit, flowers and most exotic vegetables grown in glass-houses to get an early crop, is often the produce of such rich soils; the glass-houses and polythene tunnels "lengthen" the "summer" by making it "start" earlier.

Looking across the countryside from a hill may reveal a varied way of using the land. Starting on the higher land we may see hill farms grazing sheep. Lower down may be cattle rearing for meat, beef. In more settled parts cattle may be reared and fed in a more intensive way by growing feed stuff to give them in barns or paddocks instead of grazing grass. Dairy farming with herds of cows tends to be in the richer grass meadows often in river valleys and of course it is milk and the products of milk – cream, butter, cheese – that are produced.

Arable farms are those that grow mainly crops such as wheat, barley, oats, potatoes, cabbages, kale, beet and cattle fodder crops. There are fruit farms, there are pig and poultry farms and there are the horticultural 'farms' growing carrots, onions, lettuce and tomatoes and plants and flowers.

Lastly you will see land used for other purposes than farming – for factories, for playing fields, for houses and reservoirs and gravel pits.

A landscape contains the history of the people who have lived and worked in it for centuries.

Horticulture in fertile lowlands

BE A HILL-TOP OBSERVER

If possible stand on a hill-top and look at the land around the hill.

- If you are in the northern half of England or Wales or Scotland, the tops of nearby hills may be too high or too steep to be farmed. Can you see the level on the hillsides at which the fields stop and the rough land begins?
- Lower down can you see where grazing or pasture fields end and crop-growing (arable) fields begin?
- Look in the valleys – Often the towns and villages are built in the valleys. Can you think why? Consider weather, water, rivers, road and railway lines!
- What is growing in the valleys?
- For what purposes is land used around the towns?

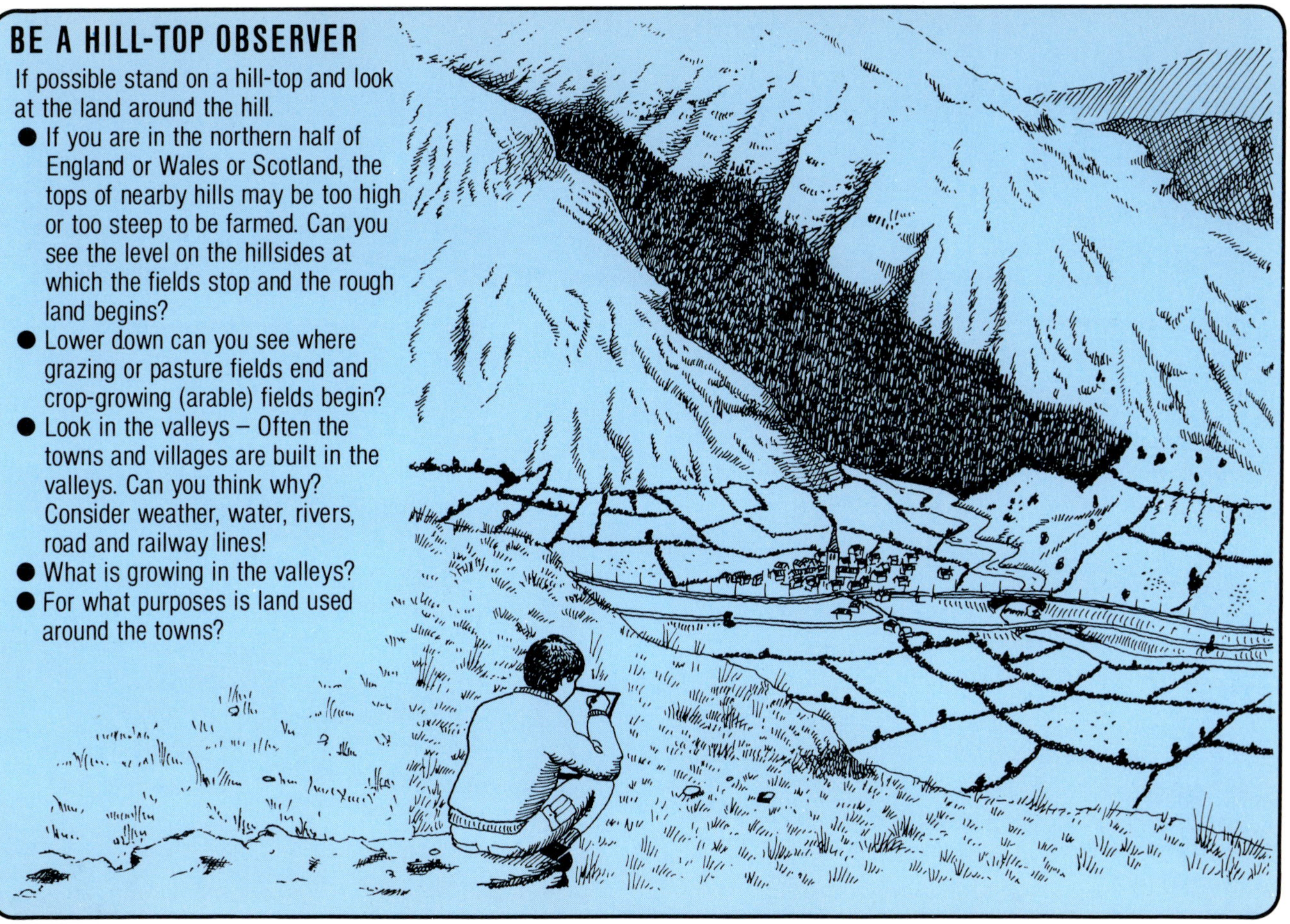

SOIL & MACHINERY

The type of landscape, what happens to the countryside and what is grown in it, usually depends in the first place on the type of soil.

Soil is important for lots of reasons. Some crops like wheat and barley need a "stiff soil" for their roots to hold them upright. Soil contains millions of bacteria – microscopic forms of life – which help to rot down dead vegetation in the soil and thus enrich it and provide food and nutrients for more plants.

Farmers must spend a lot of time improving or maintaining the richness of their soils. Keeping ditches clear and clean is obviously important to help water drainage. Sometimes buried drainage pipes are necessary and these are laid under the field. There are various machines for draining the land. The farmer must also add manures and fertilisers to his fields, and in order to know what chemicals the soil lacks he sometimes has it analysed and checked. Sometimes ditches are not dug to drain the land but to bring water to a light dry soil to irrigate it.

There are many mechanical tools which the farmer uses to prepare the soil for cultivation. Tools like the plough which turns the soil, burying unwanted vegetation, loosening and

Four Furrow Plough

If you can, visit a farm and examine the various pieces of equipment. These, and those you may see throughout the year working in the fields, can be grouped according to the type of task they perform. Try classifying those you see as follows:–
Are they used for
  a) cultivating and treating the soil
  b) planting or sowing crops
  c) treating the growing crops
  d) harvesting the crops
  e) handling or preparing the crop after harvesting
● If you are able to watch farm land regularly, keep a diary of when different equipment is used on which crops.

These are some of the different kinds of soil:
What is it where you live?
Perhaps there is more than one kind?
For instance; is the soil in the valley the same as on the hill?
See what you can find out.

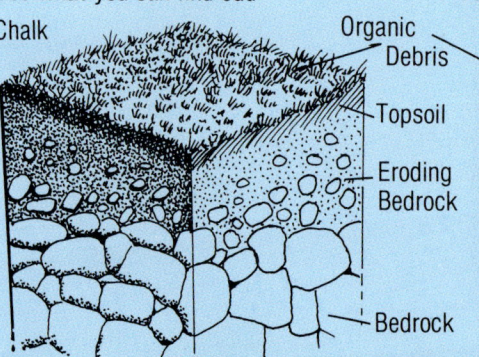

Chalk — Organic Debris — Topsoil — Eroding Bedrock — Bedrock

● **Sandy and gravelly soils:** are called 'light' soils and water passes through them easily. They warm quickly, but dry out. They need manure, decayed vegetation (humus or what the gardener calls 'compost') and often lime.

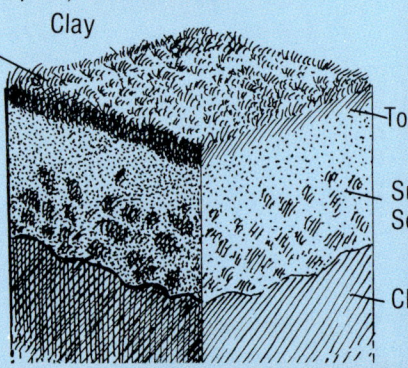

Clay — Top — Su So — Cla

Manure Spreading

used for improving the soil, for manuring, liming, fertilising, draining and irrigating. The modern farmer now has better plants that grow earlier or faster or can stand cold weather, for instance, he can now sow most of his wheat in the autumn instead of waiting for the spring. But in most things he does he is still compelled to follow the same pattern of the seasons by which the earlier farmers were controlled.

A farmer's year really starts sometime in the autumn when many crops have been harvested. First he must clear and prepare the ground, perhaps carry out some planting or sowing. Then whilst waiting for the spring, he must repair ditches, hedges, fences, buildings, trees and his equipment. As spring approaches, but according to the weather, he will start preparing the soil for the rest of the sowing and planting. During late spring and summer while crops are growing he tries to treat and protect them in various ways from weather conditions, insects and weeds. Before mid-summer he is harvesting hay which will feed his animals in the coming winter. Throughout summer into the autumn again he is harvesting more crops, and then the year starts again.

aerating the soil and preventing waterlogging; the exposed soil is then affected by frost which breaks up the lumps. Another machine ploughs with rotating blades and there are also harrows, rakes and rollers, all used to make the ground suitable for different crops. Then there are many different pieces of equipment

All the year his animals will have need of attention of different kinds for their lives, as their young are born and grow, follow the seasonal pattern also.

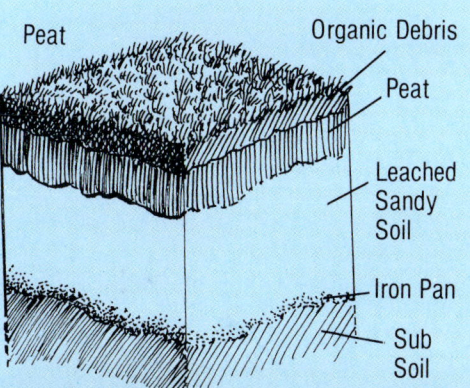

- **Clay soil:** The particles which make up clay are so microscopically small that water cannot drain through and it becomes sticky, heavy and wet. Air cannot get between the particles and it is a cold soil, slow to warm up. However, it is a good soil in a drought if crops have deep roots. When added lime and fertilisers make this a fine soil for growing.
- **Chalk and limestone soils:** drain very quickly but are sticky in wet weather, they also need manure and humus.
- **Peaty soils:** usually occur on low lying land and are rich soils for growing if well drained. They are very dark, almost black, in colour.
- **A 'loam' soil:** is a mixture of sand and clay particles; but there are different loams called heavy, medium or light loam – can you guess what makes the difference?

Peat

Organic Debris

Peat

Leached Sandy Soil

Iron Pan

Sub Soil

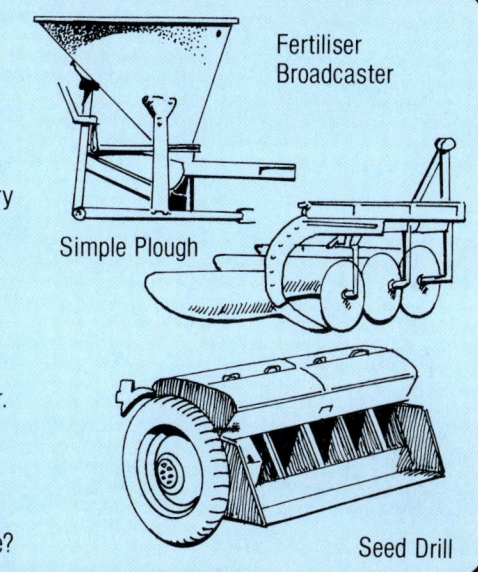

Fertiliser Broadcaster

Simple Plough

Seed Drill

NATURE'S YEAR

A field of grass can be regarded in many ways – you might think that in summer it is a place to play games, or pic-nic, or ride a horse? To a farmer it is the summer hay for winter feeding of cattle or horses; to the cattle or horses in spring it might be an immediate feast, so rich that they can become ill and even die.

To many summer butterflies and other insects a field is a vast jungle over which they fly looking for particular plants upon which they will feed or lay their eggs. The field is not

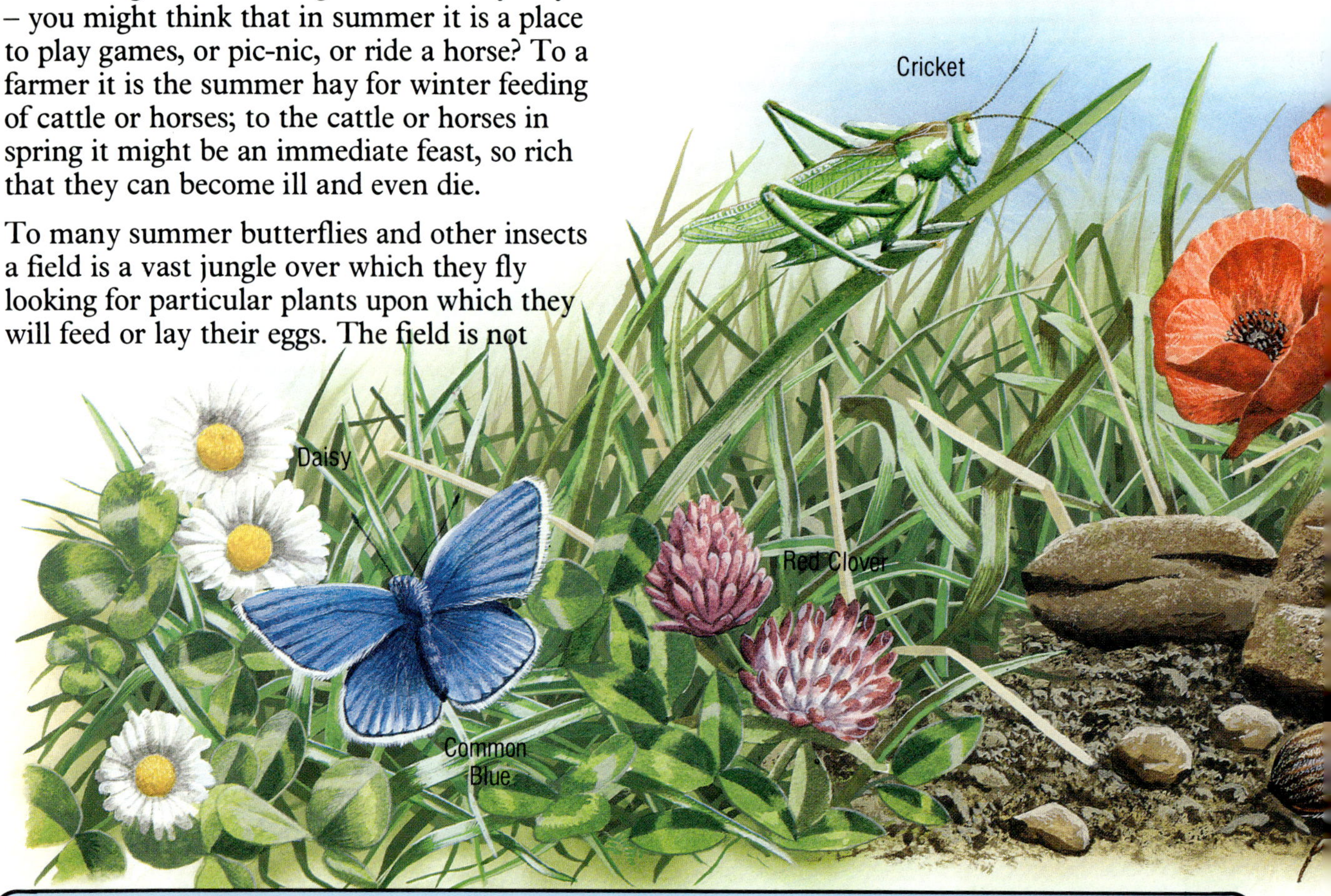

Cricket

Daisy

Red Clover

Common Blue

KEEPING A DIARY

Recording unusual events in a notebook is obviously valuable, but many important observations can pass unnoticed at the time. A solution is to keep a diary of many observations.

● Record the rare and unusual occurrences, but also the regular and relatively unimportant changes that happen.

● Dates when changes take place are interesting. When you see the first hazel catkins open; the spawning of frogs; the arrival of summer birds or the appearance of butterflies or other insects; when grasses come into flower and farmers cut hay.

● Often one happening depends upon another, and, sometimes delays of one event are disastrous upon something else.

● Record weather changes – especially when rising above or dropping below the area of 7°C or 45°F. This is about the temperature needed in the soil to cause seeds to commence growing.

● Keep a chart for each month summarising what you have written in your diary.
  Record in separate columns:–
  a) the birds you see
  b) the flowers that are in bloom
  c) the butterflies and other insects that are about
  d) whether trees are in bud or leaf or have catkins.

● Diagrams, sketches and maps can be made to illustrate your diary.

Meadow
Brown

Common
Grasshopper

Small White

Poppy

Cockchafer
Beetle

quite such a jungle of grass to rabbits and hares. Certainly some plants and grasses will be of more interest than others as favoured food, but the field will have more meaning as for them it will be a network of pathways, trackways and even "major-roads" criss-crossing in all directions. To foxes, badgers, stoats and weasels it is also a pattern of paths containing scents and signs which indicate whether prey or rivals have been around.

The activities of mammals are most clearly seen in winter when snow is on the fields. In the summer when the population of the fields is at its highest level there are predators and prey of all sizes; from the fox to the minute crab-spiders hiding in flowers and even small spiders and mites among the grass and its roots.

One scientist has calculated that in a field which was undisturbed for several years there were as many as 2 million spiders to each acre, or, nearly 4¼ million per hectare.

Imagine how many insects and other small invertebrate creatures they will consume. The same scientist also counted 500 insects caught on one spider's web in one day!

By the end of the summer a grassy field or meadow is teeming with life. The larger insects, birds and mammals that we expect to be there are all that we see in the first glance; a closer look will show the great variety of tiny creatures everywhere.

All of these creatures, small and large, have their lives affected by man the farmer, but also like the farmer, the pattern of their lives must follow the pattern of the seasons. To many town folk that pattern is often no more than – summer holidays, swimming and sun, leaves falling, rain, Christmas snow and planning summer holidays again. Perhaps if the natural changes are noticeable at all in towns it is through the trees as they become bare and then produce catkins and bursting buds before the leaves reappear.

FIELDS OF GRASS

Perhaps the most important plant in the countryside is grass. There are many kinds of grass, some of which we no longer think of as grass. The earliest farmers harvested the seeds of certain wild grasses for food.

After thousands of years of careful selection and cross breeding we now call those grasses wheat, barley and oats. Other important food crops are also grasses, for instance, rice, maize or corn, rye, the various millets and sugar cane.

In all these foods, except the last, we use the seeds of the plant. When the farmer uses grass from the fields he uses the green parts, the leaf and the stem, in two ways: either by letting his animals graze it or by cutting the grass and storing it. He cuts it, if he can, just as it is about to flower which is when it has the highest food value for the animals. We do not eat grass directly, but we do use it as food indirectly: can you think how?

The best time to look at grasses is June. This is the time when most of them begin to flower as the sufferers from "hay-fever" know. It is the pollen from the grass flowers that cause the irritation and sneezing.

Grass flowers are beautiful, especially when examined under a low powered microscope or a hand lens. The 'head' of the grass is really a cluster of lots of flowers and although there are many confusingly different forms, most can be thought of as falling into one or other of three groups according to the shape of the spike. When a complete spike is examined you will probably see some individual flowers that are not yet open, others fully open and showing the stamens able to cast pollen dust into the wind, and also flowers that have finished that stage and are beginning to grow the seeds.

Wheat   Barley   Oats

The modern farmer no longer cuts the grasses and plants that happen to grow 'wild', although sometimes he may use cattle to graze them, usually he deliberately sows selected mixtures of different grasses which suit his soil and which are best for whatever he wishes to do with the grass.

Not only the grass provides food for animals, a group of plants in the 'pea family' including the clovers and vetches are very important and their seeds are always included in the mixture of grass seeds sown by the farmer. There are lots of mixtures and varieties of clover available, but as a rough guide the short white clover is usually found in pasture fields, which are 'permanent' grassland meaning they are grazed for years.

Mixtures sown for hay or silage are called 'leys' and then the clovers used are those that grow tall and are red or pink. Silage is grass cut green – before flowering – and is not dried like hay but mixed with molasses – a raw sugar syrup – to be stored pressed down into a rich fermented 'cake' for the animals in winter. A ley is cropped once usually and therefore lasts only one or two years.

Can you understand why a farmer is angry when people trample through a "field of grass" thinking they are doing no harm?

Nowadays, except in damp meadows used for grazing and often containing buttercups, most fields of grass have been sown and it is only around the edges and along the lanes that wild flowers are to be found.

Timothy   Foxtail   Perennial Rye   Yorkshire Fog   Smooth Meadow Grass   Creeping Fescue   Yellow Oat Grass

GRASS CROPS

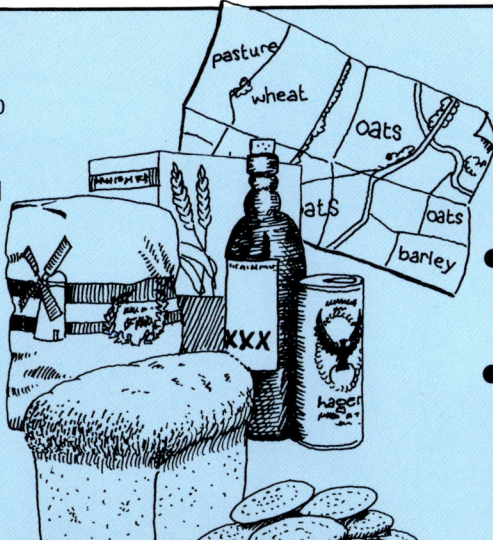

● What use is made of the grass family in the countryside nearest to where you live?
● How many fields are used for cereal crops, like wheat, barley and oats?
● What are the crops going to be used for? See if you can find out. Wheat is grown usually for flour, barley to make beer or whisky or animal feedstuffs.
Oats are used for breakfast cereal and cattle feed.
Rye for biscuits and sometimes bread.
● Find out what was grown in the same fields last year.

What is intended for next year? Different crops are grown each year as the soil is then used at different depths and the plant foods taken from the soil vary too. Some crops put nutrients back in the soil. This change of use is called "crop rotation".
● How many fields near your home are in use with grass growing for:–
a) pasture or grazing?
b) hay or silage?
● Perhaps you can now work out the type of land use of your countryside in percentages, and compare it with other areas:– a) woodland, b) arable non-grain crop, c) arable, grain crop, d) grass, hay or silage, e) grass pasture/grazing.

THRIVERS & SURVIVORS

A field growing a crop – it is either food for us or for the animals we eat – is a very "unnatural" place: it is man-made and usually for one plant only.

During the thousands of years that the farmer has grown his food he has battled with wild plants growing amongst his crops. As far as he is concerned this is the "wrong place" for them to grow and those plants are what we call "weeds".

The modern farmer using chemical "weed killer" sprays is more successful than his grandfather or even father might have been. In those days there were many plants growing

Black Bryony

Red Campion

Field Bindweed

Poppy

FLOWER DETECTIVE

Whether you know the names of many flowers or not – there are many interesting things you can find out.

- If you know a field where the grass has been grazed short – but scattered tufts and clumps of plants are also growing on it; try feeling the plants, crushing or bruising the leaves and smelling them (it is wise not to taste them). Can you decide why they have been left ungrazed and uneaten?
- Check plants into these 6 groups according to how they grow:-
  a) flat on ground – in rosettes or "runners",
  b) upright with stiff stems,
  c) supported by or leaning on other plants,
  d) scramblers with hooks or thorns or spikes,
  e) spiral stems – twisting clockwise or anti-clockwise,

  f) twisting tendrils growing from stem or leaf.
- Look out for plants that close their flowers when the sky is dull. Check them when it is sunny by using something to shade them. How much shadow is required for how long?
  What would happen to the flower in rain if it did not shut?
- Look for flowers that open at dusk; are they scented strongly? Visit them with a torch and look for moths.
- Compare the sunny side of a hedge or a roadside verge with the shady side: are there different plants on each side?
- Untwist a spiral climber and twist it the other way – check what happens later.
  Stroke an untwisted tendril a hundred times.
  Mark a climber with a tiny "twist" of metal foil so that you can measure its rate of growth each day.
- Scrape the mud from your boots into a seed tray (a metal foil food container is suitable). See how many seeds you can grow.

in the fields that are now rare or relatively uncommon: plants like Cornflower, Corn Marigold, Corn Cockle, Corn Buttercup and the red Corn Poppy, all obviously grew in the cornfields. Many of these agricultural "weeds" have almost disappeared, others only grow along the edges of roads, tracks and hedgerows and on waste ground.

Usually "weeds" are plants that were *not* common before man cleared the woodlands but they became successful because once the ground was clear they could spread their seeds prolifically and widely. Others could grow new plants easily by "creeping" from shoots along the ground, or from broken pieces of root and stem in the ground. Sometimes plants have been "successful" and have survived in pastures because cattle do not eat them; they may have prickles like the creeping thistle, or a bitter taste like the buttercup, which is also even poisonous like Ragwort.

These are the successful plants since man became a farmer – they have thrived in the bare soils of the fields. Others have only managed to survive on the edges of woods and ditches and along roads and hedges. As they are not "weeds" to the farmer, we call them wild flowers. Some, like primroses, blue bells and red campion are woodland plants and like some shade.

Many have survived by adapting themselves to scramble for light among other plants and shrubs and these are found along the hedgerows: some have tall stiff stems like the heavily scented Meadowsweet growing beside ditches and in damp corners, others have climbed up by twisting and turning or using hooks and well sprung suspenders; plants like the Bindweed, Black Bryony, Bramble, Traveller's Joy and White Bryony.

There are weak but quick growing persistent plants like the Greater Stitchwort whose white starlike flowers seem to float among the other vegetation and who climb by leaning with slender lightweight stems on other plants.

A strange survivor in the bottom of the hedge is the Cuckoo pint or pintle. A plant with many folk names like "Jack in the pulpit" it has a bulbous chamber in which it traps flies to make sure it is fertilised by another Cuckoo pint. Later it then distributes its own pollen on the flies and releases them to fly to another plant. One reason why it has survived is the fact that its roots go down as much as 50 cms.

There are many common plants along the lanes and ditches and perhaps the most confusing are the large flat headed white umbellifers. The three most common bloom one after the other from Spring to Autumn: they are the Cowparsley (May/June), Rough Chervil (June/July) and Upright Hedge Parsley (July-September). There is a fourth one, the Hogweed which is also common but it is much larger than the others.

TREE FLOWERS

The plants that most people call "flowers" are only a part of the plant world. There are many kinds of plants that do not have flowers; – such as mosses, ferns, fungi, lichens, seaweeds and others. There are others that have flowers but are not usually thought of as "flowers"; grasses and cereal plants like oats, barley and wheat have flowers as you know. All trees and shrubs are plants and almost all have flowers, including those from which we get tea, coffee and cocoa. Carrots, onions and potatoes also have flowers!

The flowers of plants become the parts in which the seeds grow and are protected until they are ripe when they are scattered from the plant. At first the seeds are called "ova" meaning eggs. However a fine microscopic dust produced by part of the flower is usually needed to start the growth of the seeds.

To do this the pollen grains must be moved to that part of the flower that contains the ova and this is called fertilisation. Most of the plants we call "flowers" and the "blossom" of fruit trees, use insects to move the pollen; but the vast majority of other trees use the wind to do this. These trees usually develop the pollen on a different flower from the one that will grow the seed. For convenience books sometimes call the pollen flower the "male" flower and the seed flower the "female". Sometimes the male and female flowers are grown near each other on the tree and sometimes on different parts of the same tree.

The flowers of most common trees are small and are best examined using a hand lens –they are then as beautiful as garden flowers.

The first catkins are usually those of the Hazel bushes growing in the hedges. February, or even January in a mild winter in the South, is the time to start looking. Knock a branch to shake the golden male catkins and you will see the yellow pollen dust. Then look closely to find the tiny green "buds" with crimson "tentacles" which are the female flowers that become hazel-nuts in September.

In March or April the willows will begin to flower. "Pussy" willow catkins – the shrub itself is called Sallow – are of two kinds. The

"Male" Catkins

Oak

Birch

"Pussy" Willow

Black Poplar

Crack Willow

silvery ones that become yellow with pollen are well known, but look at another Sallow bush for the greener catkins of the smaller female flower.

Yew trees, and the Holly, are also "male" or "female" trees and this is why berries form only on some and never on others. Look on the underside of Yew branches in early Spring, some trees will have dusty cream coloured male flowers. The trees without will have the poisonous red berries later in the year.

Many other trees have both types of flower on the same tree and some are very confusing and have different flowers (male and female) in the same flower cluster, or on separate branches, or even on separate trees and may even change from one year to the next. To help you know when to start looking the chart below shows when some of the less confusing trees begin to flower.

Crab Apple

Sycamore

	'male' & 'female' parts in the same flower	different flowers on same tree	'male' & 'female' flowers on different trees
Hazel		very early Spring	
Willows			early Spring
Poplars			early Spring
Alder		early Spring	
Yew			early Spring
Blackthorn	early Spring		
Birch		mid-Spring	
Beech		mid-Spring	
Horse Chestnut	mid-Spring		
Hawthorn	late Spring		
Oak		late Spring	
Ash		late Spring	
Holly			early Summer
Lime	early Summer		

CATKINS AND SEEDLINGS

● The seeds of some trees do not germinate or start to grow in the first spring, they wait for another year. In February or March it is worth looking near Sycamores, Horse Chestnuts, Beech or Oaks. Look under the dead leaves for seeds that appear to be splitting open – you can watch them grow.

● Seedlings, such as Sycamore, Ash and Beech produce two fleshy leaves which are different from the second pair; these later leaves are more like 'true' leaves of the tree.

OAK

● Seeds will lie in different directions but the shoots always grow up and the roots grow down. There are some ways of testing this to find out why. For these experiments, peas or beans may grow quicker than tree seeds. Place the seeds in a jar with damp blotting paper, damp sawdust, soil or sand as shown in the drawing. Prepare several jars and when the roots and shoots have started to grow, try tilting a jar or lying it on its side; try putting a jar in a closed cardboard box with a 1 cm. hole in the side. Make other holes but each day cover them all in turn except one. Look each day to see what the seedling does. Try other tests changing the light and gravity to see what happens to the shoot and the root.

COUNTRYSIDE TREES

Trees in Britain's countryside today, apart from plantations of conifers, are largely a decorative part of the landscape in most people's eyes; for the farmer they are sometimes important as shelter belts.

In the past trees were an important crop – even when growing in hedges. They were harvested in two ways. Some trees were felled, especially oak and elm and were important sources of timber for building purposes and for shipbuilding. From others a crop was taken for fuel regularly every few years – usually between 5 and 15 years. Small patches of woodland were cut to the ground and then a cluster of shoots allowed to grow up from the stump until they were a useful size as poles. This method is called "coppicing". In coppiced woodland some trees were left to grow to full height as timber trees. Coppiced trees needed to be enclosed to prevent cattle, horses and deer from eating the young growth.

One way to avoid this problem was to cut the tree but leave a trunk of between 2 or 3 metres instead of a stump. This practice is called "pollarding". By this method the young wood grew at a height beyond the reach of browsing animals and is why we have these characteristically shaped trees in hedges and alongside streams.

Another method of obtaining wood is to regularly remove all the side branches. The tree grows taller as the top is left but the cut branches provide a source of useful wood. This practice, called "shredding", is not used very much today, but coppiced stumps and pollard trees are still common throughout the countryside.

Hazel, a native shrub is common as a coppice and is popular because of the nuts it produces.

The Sweet Chestnut, introduced by the Romans, is often coppiced in woods but not usually found in hedgerows. In Europe this chestnut is grown as a full tree along roads and fields and it then provides the chestnuts which we roast. In Britain, the summer is not usually suitable to produce good chestnuts from our trees.

An attractive tree, often only seen as a shrub is the Field Maple; it does not usually produce the brilliant colours for which the American maples are famous but during a warm autumn changes from lemon yellows through golden shades to orange pinks, and even a subtle scarlet. The related Great Maple or Sycamore has a similar shaped but much larger leaf.

Wild Service

Spindle Fruit

Perhaps most common as trees in our countryside, apart from the oak, are the elm and the ash. The English Elm, which has suffered so much from the "Dutch elm disease", has a billowing crown above a straight trunk and used to be more common in southern Britain, it is replaced in the north by the Wych Elm that has a shorter trunk and larger leaf. Both Wych Elm and Common Ash tend to occur more frequently on higher, exposed sites than the oak.

Also in hilly country look out for the Rowan or Mountain Ash (not a true Ash). Unusual trees to look for in the countryside are the Spindle, the Wild Service tree, the Wild Cherry and the small-leaved Lime.

TREE STUDY

Why not make a book about the trees where you live?

- Start with a few common trees.
- You can then collect and press the leaves and mount them in your book.
- Find out what the flowers or catkins are like – you may be able to press them too.
- Draw and sketch the twigs and flowers, or, in the Winter, the shape of the tree with its branches against the sky.
- You can make patterns with bark rubbings, leaf rubbings, leaf prints and spatter prints and mount these in your book.
- The seeds of your trees can be grown in pots.
- Measure the height of the trees, the girth around the trunks, and the area covered by their shadows at different times.
- Record other information: when do the buds open, when do the flowers appear and when do the leaves fall?

- There are books to help identify species and provide you with more information to write into your book. For instance, what is the timber of the tree used for?

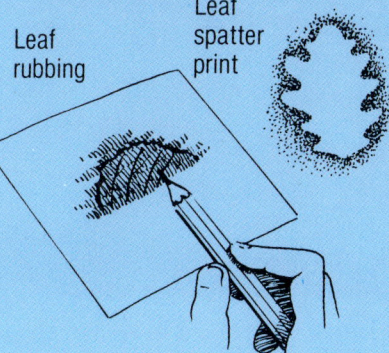
Leaf rubbing
Leaf spatter print

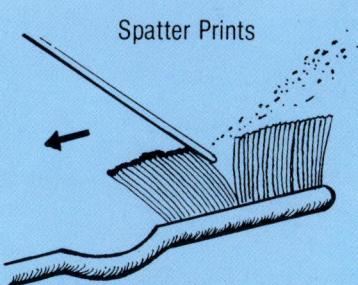
Spatter Prints

LEAF RUBBING: Place a leaf on a table with the underside uppermost. Cover it with a piece of paper and then rub the paper above the leaf evenly with a wax crayon. You can add to the effect by applying a colour wash afterwards. Choose a typical example to add to your book.

BARK RUBBING: This is a similar process, but on a larger scale; with some help from a friend, hold the paper against the tree and rub evenly with the crayon. The paper should be larger and strong. Afterwards cut out the most characteristic piece of your pattern to stick in your book.

SPATTER PRINTS: Place the leaf on the paper, then, using an old tooth brush dipped in wet paint, "spatter" evenly around the leaf by drawing a piece of wood or a pencil towards you across the bristles of the brush. Sometimes this can be combined with leaf rubbings.

WOODS & HEDGES

Hedges mark the boundaries between fields and sometimes between parishes. In some parts of the countryside the hedges have been there since the fields were first cleared out of the surrounding woodland. We know this from the plants that grow in the hedgerows as well as from very old records. When hedges are growing on a mounded bank, usually accompanied by a large hollow ditch, they are often ancient boundaries between the land of one village and that of the next. Often these boundaries are an irregular line on the map, in contrast to the pattern of other hedgerows. Sometimes there is a wood adjoining the boundary and usually this is very ancient too. In some parts of the country stone walls or dykes mark the boundaries. In other places, hedges, walls or fences, especially if their line is straight and orderly, are later in history and indicate a change of use or a social change and change of ownership.

It might be part of a Roman road or an old packhorse route, or an ancient bridleway or footpath. Sometimes it may be an old road (before roads were given hard surfaces), called a green lane, along which cattle were driven to graze or even to market over long distances by men called "drovers". These are all that is left of the "drove-roads" or "cattle-drift ways" that were used all over Europe long before the cowboys made their cattle trails across America.

Surfaced roads, as we know them, are less than a hundred years old and some of the old trackways and lanes have been surfaced to take motor vehicles. When roads twist and turn and have steep banks or they are sunken below the level of the fields they run between, they give clues showing their ancient past. The banks and hedges of these old lanes are also often rich in wild flowers and many kinds of shrub.

Wild Garlic or "Ransomes"

Bluebells

Primroses

Most early hedges date from Saxon times or, at least 600, 700 or even 800 years ago, from Medieval times. The later hedges may be between 250 and 150 years old from the period when the open common land of the villages passed into the hands of large landowners.

A double hedgerow, with a track or path between the hedges is sometimes an old route.

There are some plants that tell us whether hedges or woods are likely to be very old. The little green flowered Dog's Mercury is a good "indicator". It is a woodland plant that spreads very slowly and prefers undisturbed soil. If it is found in a hedge bottom it may be that the hedge was once part of old woodland.

Woods with carpets of Bluebells or Primroses are usually old, especially if there is a rich

COUNTRYSIDE DETECTIVE

Maybe your local hedgerows or woods and copses are old, perhaps they have been coppiced or pollarded. Or, perhaps they were just awkward corners not worth ploughing and were left for pheasants to nest in or to provide a place from where the local Hunt could drive a fox. They may have been deliberately planted to provide timber or shelter for crops.

How old is your countryside? There are many clues which will help you find out.

Lanes and smaller roads:– are they straight or twisting? Do they have tall banks and many flowers? Are they sunken?

Hedges:– are they double with a trackway or path? Are they straight or irregular and twisting? Do they contain many species of shrubs? Are they growing on a mound or bank? Is there a ditch alongside that does not appear to drain water? Are there woodland plants growing in the hedge?

Footpaths:– where do they go and why do you think they were used? Examine a local map.

Old Woods:– is the shape irregular? Are the edges curved and the corners rounded?
- does any edge have a large round-topped bank with a broad ditch outside it?
- is it adjoining the parish boundary or in a far corner of the parish and on poor soil?
- does it contain many species of tree? (esp. Crab, Hazel, Holly, Wild Service, Hornbeam, Woodland Hawthorn).
- does it have many different woodland flowers and not a predominance of ivy or cow parsley?
- are the trees of different ages and scattered about and not in rows and all about the same age?

A scientist called Dr. Max Hooper has discovered that:– if you count the species of woody shrubs and trees growing in a 28 metre length of hedge, the age of the hedge in hundreds of years is usually the same as the number of species of shrub or tree. That is on average one new species occurs by accident every 100 years.

It is wise to test several 28 metre stretches and then take an average.

mixture of other plants too, like the Cuckoo pint, Yellow-dead nettle, or Wood anemone. Rarer plants such as the various orchids and Butcher's Broom also only occur in woods that have been in existence for a long time. Widespread growth of Cow Parsley or Ivy in a wood will often mean it is not an old wood but quite recent in origin. Of the trees in a piece of woodland, generally speaking, if they vary greatly in age – very old trees scattered among younger trees – and trees of a variety of species, then the wood is likely to be old. However, it can still be old if it has been coppiced even if big old trees are not present. If a wood contains Crab apple trees, the Wild Service, or the native Small-leaved Lime as well then it is certainly a piece of ancient woodland.

Cuckoo Pint

Sweet Chestnut

BUTTERFLIES

One of the most noticeable effects of modern changes in the countryside is the decrease in numbers of butterflies. No one knows for certain why but there are several probable causes, such as the spread of towns; the mechanisation of the farms which has meant a more "tidy" countryside with less wild and rough corners for different food plants to grow. Weed killer chemicals have reduced food plants still more and insecticides have no doubt affected the butterflies themselves.

It is through butterflies that most people find out about the various stages in an insect's life. Butterflies like many insects have four stages: the egg, the caterpillar or larvae, then the chrysallis or pupae and finally the adult butterfly.

The eggs are difficult to find or see usually, being very small. The Large White butterfly's eggs are sometimes found on the underside of cabbage leaves, or, in May when the Orange-tip butterfly is flying along the lanes by searching the two food plants, Lady's Smock and Jack-by-the-hedge. It is less painful to watch for a Small Tortoiseshell to lay eggs on a head of stinging nettles rather than search through a whole patch of nettles!

Butterflies have a long sucking tube, usually called its tongue, which you can see coiled up like a spring under the head. This is used to suck the nectar out of flowers – the only food the butterfly eats. Watch butterflies on flowers to see this.

The caterpillar has very powerful biting or chewing jaws: using a lens watch a caterpillar feeding on a leaf. Caterpillars also have, just behind their mouths, a spinneret with which they can make silk. Usually four times during their period as a caterpillar, they spin a silk pad to which they cling whilst shedding their

In the past it has been popular to make collections of butterflies, but now that many are so scarce this could be harmful and reduce numbers still more. It is more fun to rear them and release them knowing that perhaps some of those you see during the following days or next year are the ones you reared!

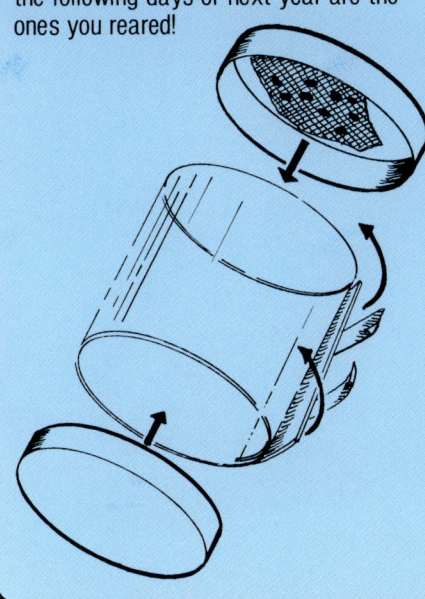

REARING CATERPILLARS

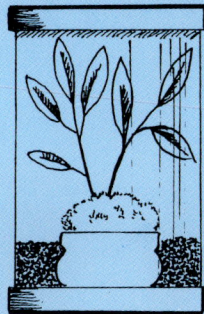

- There are several ways of rearing caterpillars. Perhaps the best way to watch events is to use a large round biscuit or coffee tin. Knock some holes in the lid with a nail but glue a piece of nylon stocking over the holes to keep the caterpillars in and parasitic flies and wasps out.
- You need a strip of clear acetate at least 30 cm. wide and long enough to go round the tin with an overlap which you can secure with sellotape. (Assemble as in the illustration.)

- Fill the tin about 3 cm. deep with peaty soil – as many moth caterpillars pupate in the soil – and place a small jar in the peat, containing water and sprigs of the food plant. Plug the top of the jar with some cotton wool to prevent the caterpillars drowning.
- Peacock or Small Tortoiseshell caterpillars found and fed on stinging nettles are the best to start with. They will pupate on the nettle stems or the lid and after 2 or 3 weeks the butterflies will emerge and dry their wings while hanging from the twig.
- A damp pad of cotton wool smeared with a little honey, or a pad moistened with sugar water will keep the butterflies alive if you are not there when they emerge.
- A chrysallis which needs to over-winter must be kept outside in cool, damp conditions in a closed box or tin. In the spring replace it in your "cage" with some twigs to which the new insect can cling.

skin. On the fifth occasion it is usually the chrysallis that emerges from the old skin. Whereas the caterpillar stage was a feeding and growing period, the chrysallis stage is a resting and changing time.

Some butterflies spend the winter as a chrysallis, but other species wait as hibernating or torpid caterpillars until the spring. There are other kinds that over-winter in the egg stage and a group of others that hibernate as grown adult butterflies.

Because of these differences some butterflies live only for a month or so, whilst others live for almost a year.

By rearing butterflies from eggs or caterpillars it is possible to watch the various stages in their lives. Most amazing – if you are fortunate enough to see it – is the emergence

of the butterfly from the pupal case. The wings are small, soft and crumped up. The insect must get clear of the case before the wings are "pumped-up" by a liquid from the body. This usually takes half an hour and within another hour the wings are hard and the butterfly can fly. The antennae are sense organs that assist in balance. Most butterflies have six legs of which the third pair are also sense organs by which the insect can taste and detect the food plant.

If you find a dead butterfly, examine its wings carefully with a lens. The "colouring" comes off – look at the coloured "dust" for it consists of thousands of tiny scales. There are different shaped scales on different parts of the wing and different shapes on different species of butterfly. Examine the scales on a piece of "sellotape".

Small white   Tortoiseshell   Common Blue   6 spot Burnet Moth

INSECT FAMILIES

Although butterflies are spectacular insects, the fields, meadows and hedgerows are full of many other small creatures, less noticeable but living quite remarkable lives, some of which we do not fully understand.

At first you will notice bees and wasps and flies, or, if you look closely at leaves – underneath them as well as on top – you will see creatures that crawl rather than fly. How do you begin to distinguish them? The chart opposite shows the obviously different groups based on the number of legs. Other structural differences and details, such as how many pairs of wings or the precise pattern of veins on the wings require a close examination only possible by catching the creature. However, much can be seen by carefully stalking closer and closer. It is especially easy on a warm

Hoverfly

Weevil

Leaf cutting Bee

Ichneumon Wasp

Hoverfly Larvae

Lacewing Eggs

Green Lacewing

Aphids

windy day, as presumably with the movement of vegetation a moving observer is not so noticeable.

There are a number of clues which help you make an approximate identification. Round furry insects are usually wild bumble bees. Honey bees are not so furry and although varying in colour, are usually pale brown and black and look like a stocky wasp. There are two common yellow and black wasps –

Buff-tailed Bumble Bee

Ox-eye Daisy

Spittlebugs

Nettle

Scorpion Fly

Stripe-Winged Grasshopper

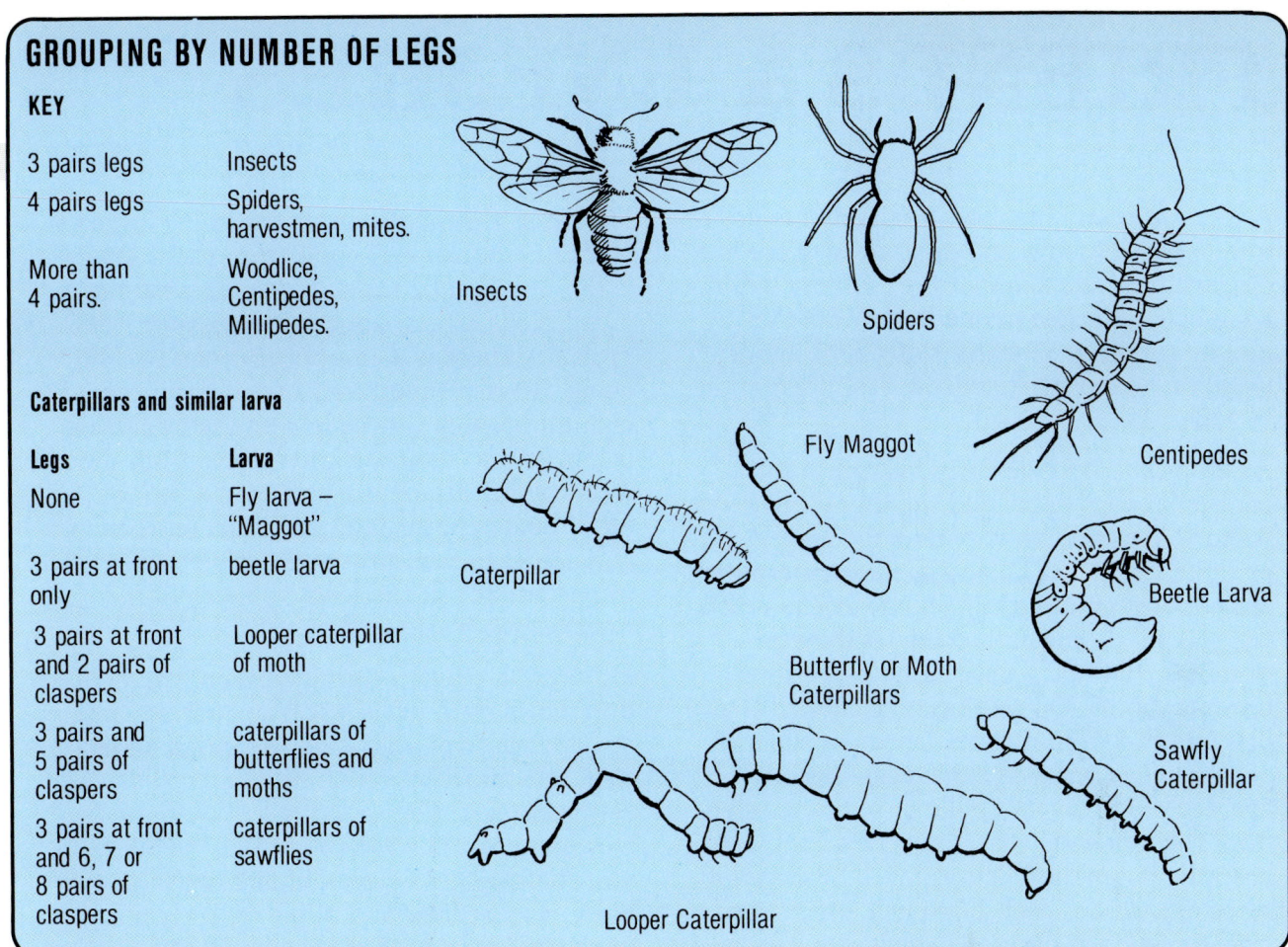

GROUPING BY NUMBER OF LEGS

KEY

3 pairs legs	Insects
4 pairs legs	Spiders, harvestmen, mites.
More than 4 pairs.	Woodlice, Centipedes, Millipedes.

Caterpillars and similar larva

Legs	Larva
None	Fly larva – "Maggot"
3 pairs at front only	beetle larva
3 pairs at front and 2 pairs of claspers	Looper caterpillar of moth
3 pairs and 5 pairs of claspers	caterpillars of butterflies and moths
3 pairs at front and 6, 7 or 8 pairs of claspers	caterpillars of sawflies

Insects

Spiders

Fly Maggot

Centipedes

Caterpillar

Beetle Larva

Butterfly or Moth Caterpillars

Sawfly Caterpillar

Looper Caterpillar

distinguished by the markings on the face – but several other kinds of wasps, whilst not looking like their larger relatives are true wasps. Many make individual nests for their eggs and larvae, and these are called "solitary" wasps.

"Wasps" that hover are usually Hoverflies which by mimicing the wasp's colouring gain protection from its reputation though they themselves are harmless.

"Flies" with rather long bodies but without any waist at all are often Sawflies, so called because their egg laying tube has developed a "saw" by which they cut into the stems of plants to lay their eggs.

Long bodied "flies" with constantly moving antennae and very narrow waists are usually members of the wasp family. They are Ichneumon wasps and are parasitic upon other insects. There are thousands of different kinds and each one lays eggs on or inside the body of its own particular species of insect "host" – eventually, after the ichneumon's eggs have hatched its larva start eating the host insect from the inside, it dies finally as the ichneumon larva are ready to pupate.

Ichneumons are often dark with orange or yellow legs and rapid movements.

"Useful" insects fall into three groups (useful to man, that is): those that pollinate trees and crops, those that are hunters and killers (predators) of pest creatures and those that are scavengers (feeding on dead remains). Of the predators, probably the Ladybird beetle is the best known; both the adult beetle and the larvae feed on aphids and other plant pests. Adult Robberflies feed on the nectar of flowers but the larva of many species are carnivores feeding on other insects whilst some are scavengers. Larva of the Lacewing flies are also useful predators of pests. Adult scorpion flies are both predators and scavengers.

Most of the harmful insects are plant eaters and as a general rule move more slowly than predatory creatures. Aphids (greenfly and blackfly, etc.), various plant bugs, weevils, the larva of many beetles and the cranefly or "daddy-long-legs" larva, also well known as "leatherjackets", are some of the worst offenders. Many eat the plant as it grows but others like the "leatherjacket" feed on the roots.

FRIENDS & ENEMIES

A tree has many branches which divide up into a mass of twigs and on each twig are lots of leaves. By late summer few of these will not have been attacked in one way or another by insects and bugs of many kinds. One small wood or hedgerow contains a vast population of such creatures.

As the leaves open in early May millions of caterpillar eggs hatch and the tiny moth larva begin to feed and grow among the leaves. Two or three weeks later many of these caterpillars are pupating in rolled up leaves, others reach the ground on silken threads. Of the vast numbers that hatch only a tiny proportion become moths. One biologist calculated that just one pair of moths can be responsible for producing as many as 2,000 eggs. But on average only two caterpillars need to survive until the following year, to become moths, to keep the population figures level. Some 1,998 caterpillars from each 2,000 will, on average, provide food for birds and predatory insects between one spring and the next!

However, this invertebrate (meaning animals without a backbone) population of the leaves is not one chaotic mass of creatures eating away at the tree or each other without "rules" – there is a complicated pattern. To avoid direct competition some creatures feed or hunt by night, some live on the underside of the leaves, some suck the juices from the stem, others attack the buds and a host of other kinds appear later and feast on the fruits and seeds. In fact, timing is perhaps the most important key in the whole pattern of this interlocking world.

Different creatures eating different meals need different mouth parts – it is by looking closely at these that you may find out much about each one. Start by watching a caterpillar eating away at the edge of a leaf with its chewing jaws. A wasp (in a tube) will show you chewing jaws also, and although the wasp bites away at fruit and other vegetation and even scrapes at bark, dead wood and fence posts to chew wood into the papier-mâché

Mottled Umber

Yellow Tail Caterpillar

Peppered Moth Caterpillar

Hoverfly

Pale Tussock Moth Caterpillar

Fox Moth Caterpillar

Wood Ant

Oak Eggar Moth

Large White
Plume Moth

Long Horned Moth

Brown
China-Mark

Mother
Shipton

Dot
Moth

Brown
Moth

Common
Quaker

Vapourer

which is used to build the wasp colony's nest, the wasp also uses its biting jaws to scavenge. In dry summers wasps can be seen feeding on the corpses of dead insects and animals.

There are numerous kinds of plant bugs equipped with long piercing mouth parts. Most of them sink their dagger-like beaks into plants to suck out the juices, but a few are carnivorous and feed on other creatures, such as caterpillars and aphids. Aphids are worth a close look with a lens; like the larger capsid and shield bugs, they have a long sharp "beak" folded back under their "chin" and this is a sucking tube. The froghopper or spittle bug creates a protective froth from the plant's juices after they have passed through its body. Some flies have biting mouth parts and others have a flat sucking pad – look closely at a house fly. Snakeflies, scorpion flies, hover flies, lacewings and several beetles have larva which in most cases are fierce carnivores with strong biting jaws or pincers.

Not only are there dangers among the leaves but the air immediately above the tree is sometimes hawked by swooping swallows and swifts skimming the foliage, taking insects flying about the leaves. On the bark of the tree in nooks and crannies are other predators such as spiders and beetles, while down on the ground under the tree is another mini-world.

BE A MINI-EXPLORER
● Where to look for insects:–
Under leaves as well as on top. Behind loose bark and in cracks and crannies.
Inside lumps and bumps (galls) growing on leaves, twigs and buds – cut them open carefully!
● What to look with:–
Use a hand lens (x8 is powerful enough) – these can be purchased at opticians or shops selling optical equipment.
● How to look:–
Hold your lens close to your eye, resting your hand on your cheek. Slowly move the object you wish to examine towards your eye until it is in focus.

● How to catch and collect:–
Careful stalking and very slow movement using a glass or plastic tube with a plastic cap. (Ask your parents for an empty pill container). For "lucky-dip" collecting you need two friends, a piece of white sheet (about 1 metre square), lots of jars and tubes. Your friends should hold

the sheet beneath a low branch which you should knock sharply and suddenly with a stick. Collect everything that falls quickly – sort and examine later.
Turn to page 43 to see how to make a "sweep-net" which is another way of collecting.

FRIENDS OR FOES

Birds of many kinds are noticeable on a country walk, but many of them are using the fields and meadows as feeding grounds and actually nest and roost elsewhere.

Lack of nest sites may be much more important than we sometimes think. Many of the most useful birds as far as the farmer is concerned need trees for nesting and the loss of elms by the 'dutch elm-disease' and the removal of hedges may have a considerable effect.

Two owls – the Little and the Barn owl – occur in countryside rather than woodland and both use holes in trees as nest sites. years ago farmers, when building a barn often included a high entrance for the Barn owl. A wise farmer today will put a large box in the roof of an open barn with 15 cm. entrance hole and a layer of sawdust. Both owls take a large number of mice and voles and harmful beetles in their diet.

The Kestrel, another wholly beneficial bird-friend of the farmer, nests in holes in trees or old crow's nests in trees.

Two other birds which on the whole do more good than harm, the Rook and the Jackdaw, also depend on tall trees for nest sites: many Rookeries in the past have been built in groups of elms. The Jackdaw also tends to be gregarious, several pairs nesting in hollow trees in close proximity.

Both Rooks and Jackdaws feed in large flocks, sometimes numbering hundreds, moving to the fields as soon as the family parties are strong enough to fly. The large flocks are then a common sight through Autumn and Winter. Jackdaws can be distinguished in the flocks by their slightly smaller size and faster wing beat. Wireworms, leather jackets and other harmful grubs form a large part of their diet and although they also eat quantities of grain, most of this is from the stubble after harvesting.

The Carrion Crow, which is not gregarious like the Rook, is considered to be more of a villain because although it takes harmful insects and mammals it will also take chicks and attack young lambs. Another member of the crow family, the Magpie, is thought to do rather more good for the farmer than harm, however, because Magpies destroy large numbers of other birds' eggs and young, many of them being insect-eating birds, the Magpie like the Jay is considered a menace to wild-life when it is present in large numbers.

Rook and Woodpigeons

There is often a conflict of interest between the farmer and the gamekeeper. Several birds and animals, like the Owl, the Kestrel, the Jay,

Male Kestrel

the Magpie, the fox, the stoat and weasel are thought of as enemies by the gamekeeper who is trying to protect his pheasant chicks, but because they take small mammals and harmful insects they are friends of the farmer.

One of the most useful birds on the land is the Lapwing, large flocks of these plovers occur in the late summer – sometimes these are gatherings of local birds but by Autumn they could be birds preparing to migrate southwards and westwards or arrivals from Europe.

Often in the same fields are parties of Blackheaded and Common Gulls and it is obvious that they can be looked upon as friends by the farmer by the way they follow the plough looking for insect larva turned up with the soil.

The greatest villain at all times is the Woodpigeon: not only does it eat grain, peas and green crops, but it has an enormous appetite. Large flocks sometimes occur in Winter and whole fields of cabbages or Brussels sprouts can then be ruined in hours.

BIRD-WATCH

Bird watching in the open countryside is in some ways more difficult than in woodland, as birds may not allow you to come very close and can see you from farther away.

- Binoculars are particularly useful but field craft will also help you to see more. Never enter a field without first searching it with your binoculars, scan too the hedges, trees or walls around the field. Make use of a bank or rise in the ground as concealment. Walk beside the hedge or wall rather than into the open field, keep quiet and move slowly.

- A field note-book is most important: do not trust your memory but make notes immediately. Note details such as how the bird flies – slow or rapid wing beats, straight and even flight, or dipping up and down, wings with "fingers" or pointed wing tips?

Keep a diary going too because the date that you see something can be important.

- When counting a large flock, count ten birds and then estimate how many groups of ten make up the flock – it is usually more than you expect!
- In winter record numbers and the direction of bird flocks in flight. You may discover there are regular flight-lines; such as Rooks and Jackdaws or Starlings, just before sunset. You may notice, a regular direction or movement of birds when there is a marked weather change; watch for Lapwings.

HEDGEROW BIRDS

Very few small birds live entirely in the fields, with the exception of the Skylark and the Meadow Pipit, but birds such as the Chaffinch, Goldfinch, Bullfinch, Yellowhammer, Whitethroat, Willow Warbler and parties of foraging tits are usually found along the hedgerows, lanes or woods of the countryside.

Sometimes it is possible to see only a glimpse of the bird as it flits along a hedge. On these occasions there are useful clues that help you to identify the bird. Suppose as the bird flies along the hedge all you can see is a brown back with a bright chestnut rump (the back above the tail where the wings fold) and white feathers on the outside edge of the tail. In such a case the bird would almost certainly be a Yellowhammer. If the bird had white on the outer edge of the tail, no brown back but a lot of white on the wings it would be a Chaffinch. Or, if you could see nothing very distinctive except a bright white rump patch, it is most likely to be a Bullfinch. Sometimes one or two recognition points like this are sufficient to identify many common birds once you know the only other possibility is something much more rare.

On seeing a strange bird, try to decide its size compared with a bird you know. What does its general appearance suggest to you – what other bird is it like? Ask yourself is it slim and slender or round and fluffy – but remember a bird's shape can change with weather conditions or whether it feels aggressive or not. Do not forget that colours too can change and vary with the light. There are some clues that are particularly conspicuous, for instance, the white rump of the bullfinch, the two white wing bars on the chaffinch and yellow bar on the wings of the goldfinch. Notice the outer tail feathers, some birds have these prominently white, for example the reed bunting and yellowhammer. Learn to describe a bird in your notebook by the names of parts of its body, and write down what you see immediately the bird has flown away. Do it before you look in a book, because what you read may influence your memory.

There are other points to notice; was the tail long or short; was it square, forked, rounded or wedge shaped; was the flight straight or dipping up and down; did the bird hop, walk or run? Soon you will begin to notice these characteristics without effort.

RECORDING UNUSUAL BIRDS

Size		The same as a:– Sparrow? Blackbird? Pigeon?
Shape	General	slim, slender, squat, rounded?
	Wings	rounded, pointed?
	Tail	long, short, square or forked?
	Legs	long or short, colour?
	Beak or Bill	curved, long, hooked, pointed, etc.?
Colour	General	of the breast, back, wings, tail?
	Other Markings	wing bars; tail, rump, eye stripe, crest, cap, 'bib'?
Flight		direct or up and down, rapid, slow or fluttering?
Gait		running, walking, hopping?
Behaviour		sulking, bold, shy?

Prominent "in flight" checkpoints to look for in small common birds of hedges and woods.

Wingmarkings	white	Chaffinch
	yellow	Goldfinch, Siskin, Greenfinch
Rump	white	Bullfinch, Brambling, House Martin
	yellow	Siskin
	chestnut	Yellowhammer
Tail-outer feathers	white	Chaffinch, Yellowhammer, Reed Bunting, Great Tit, Pipits and Wagtails, Common Whitethroat
Tail patches	yellow	Greenfinch, Siskin
Little or no prominent markings:–		most Warblers, Dunnock, Wren, Robin, Sparrow

Cuckoo

Redwing

Dunnock

Lapwing

Fieldfare

31

FEATHERS, FUR & FEET

Dead Great tit

Sometimes you may learn from tragedies. Casualties on country roads are sometimes the only chance you will have of examining some birds at close range. Such deaths are to be regretted, but remember many natural predators are extinct or rare now and humans with their cars are in a sense, a balancing hazard that takes the predators place.

The wildlife victims of road accidents are usually "fresh" because there are plenty of scavenging birds such as crows and magpies and at night patrolling foxes looking for this kind of meal and thus a corpse is quickly removed.

However, the unfortunate victim provides us with a chance to examine feet, beaks, wings and feathers.

In this way you will quickly acquire the ability to recognise the occasional isolated feather or a single tuft of fur that you may find on a walk. For instance, although the hair of a fox and a hare are similar in colour the fox has a dark underfur, whilst that of the hare is fleecy white. A patch of scattered feathers on the ground that tells you a kill has been made should be looked at closely. Whether the feathers are plucked or appear to be 'cut with scissors' is the difference between the work of the beak of a bird of prey or a fox's teeth.

FINDING FEATHER FACTS

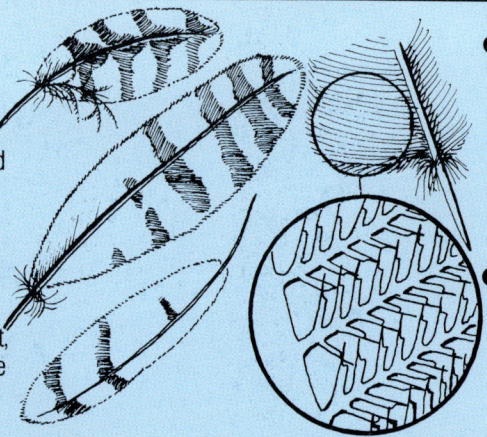

Feathers are meant to overlap other feathers and the body feathers thus protect the layer of small down feathers that are close to the skin, and surround the bird with warm air. The wing and tail feathers must overlap to stop air passing through in flight.

● Examine a wing of a dead bird; the feathers part and allow air through as the spread wing is on the upbeat, but as the bird beats downward the wing feathers are pressed together to make flight possible.

● The individual "strands" of a feather are each equipped with a row of hooks which act rather like zip-fasteners. A split in the feather's surface can be repaired by stroking it between thumb and finger. A bird does this with its beak when preening.

● The smaller wing feathers – the coverts – cover the holes at the base of the main flight feathers. Examine these small feathers and compare them with the back and breast feathers. It is interesting to

Look at the feet of a dead fox by the roadside and you will see a thick tuft of hair growing between the pads of each foot – a dog does not have this. Look also at the fox's claws for they will be sharp like a cats, not blunt like those of a dog. A fox's footprint in the mud may show the sharp marks of the claws and also the imprint of the tuft of hair.

If you are travelling in a car at night watch for a bold fox crossing the road in the headlights. At any time of day or night a weasel or stoat may dart across the road. The stoat will have a rippling bound and a longish black-tipped tail, whereas a weasel's long straight body appears to zoom across the road as if its feet are not there; its tail is so short it will not be very noticeable.

Weasel

Mole, Magpie and Weasel – victims of a gamekeeper

If a roadside victim is a bird, look at the wing and tail feathers. These are the largest feathers on the bird and have a stiff shaft running down them. The wing feathers and outer tail feathers have one edge narrower than the other, depending upon the side of the body from which it comes. Perhaps the feathers most commonly found are those from the Wood Pigeon; its dark grey wing feathers are edged with white, its tail feathers are banded, black, white and grey whilst its smaller blue-grey body feathers are easily recognised by the thick white down at their base. Large black and white feathers in the fields are likely to be from a magpie or a lapwing, also called a 'pee-wit'. A delicate, wispy and 'furry' feather, coloured in browns, grey and cream usually means a Tawny Owl has been along the hedgerow or through the wood.

Pheasant and Partridge feathers are similarly coloured but not furry like the owl.

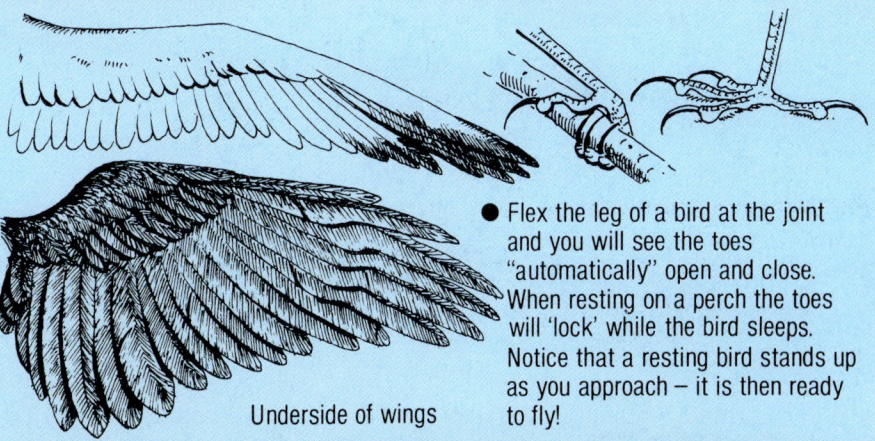

make a collection of different feathers from different species of bird. You can make a quiz to see if your friends can not only name the bird but say from which part of the body each feather comes.

● It is a simple matter to collect the wings of all except large birds, as the wing dries out without any unpleasant smell. Open the wing and snip it at a joint. If pinned open on a piece of board or card for a few weeks, it will remain in the open position.

Underside of wings

● Flex the leg of a bird at the joint and you will see the toes "automatically" open and close. When resting on a perch the toes will 'lock' while the bird sleeps. Notice that a resting bird stands up as you approach – it is then ready to fly!

NOCTURNAL HUNTERS

Pair of Badgers

The dominance of man throughout the landscape is possibly one of the reasons why some of the larger animals only come out to feed at night. Certainly the fox becomes active at dusk, hunts throughout the night and retires to rest at dawn in its "earth" or a dense thicket. Even young fox cubs reared in captivity and quiet all day become very active and playful at dusk. The fox, like other night hunters the dog and the cat (although now domesticated) has eyes that are able to see in the dark much more effectively than our eyes. This is achieved by a layer of reflecting cells in the eye and it is this that makes them glow in the headlights of a car. Test your dog at night – he will see you when you cannot see him; shine a torch on his face from a distance.

The badger, with striking white, black and grey markings is clearly a night hunter, but 'brock' is out looking for worms, slugs, snails, beetles and any of the other small creatures of the woodland floor. They emerge to eat the vegetation – living or dead – after the heat has gone from the air and when its moisture level is greater and the ground is often wet with dew. Most of these creatures will die if exposed in a day time atmosphere. In times of drought snails will completely seal up the

Fox

opening of their shell and worms will burrow deep down into the soil.

Also snuffling around at night for worms and night insects is the hedgehog which in turn may fall victim to the fox or even badger. Foxes manage to kill and eat the hedgehog, often only leaving the prickly skin turned inside out. On at least one occasion a fox has been observed taking a curled up hedgehog and dropping it in water to force it to uncurl and thus enable the fox to bite the underside where there are no spines.

Noctule Bat

Most ingenious in locating each other in the dark are the males and females of the beetle we call the glow-worm. Although the male can fly the female is flightless and compared to the male's dim effort gives off a very bright light from the hind end of her body by a mixture of chemical substances. Glow-worms feed on snails which are active and easy to find at night. As dawn approaches the night watch retires to bed and the day shift comes on.

Garden Tiger Moth

Elephant Hawk Moth

Bats are night hunters too, flying above the trees and through the woodland glades. Their food is largely moths. Although butterflies are only active during daylight hours (diurnal) most moths are nocturnal. From dusk onwards many of the larger moths will be visiting night opening flowers, probing with their long tongues to reach the sugary nectar deep in the flower. These flowers attract the moths to assist in pollination often because they are pale in colour, but more effectively over great distances by scent to which moths are very sensitive. It is by emitting scent that the female of some species attracts the male – in some cases, it is said he will come from up to a mile away.

COUNTRYSIDE NIGHT WATCH

Night-watching can be breathtakingly exciting, but you should be prepared properly beforehand.

- Take a companion who is as keen as you are and knows how to be quiet. Also make sure your parents know.
- Choose a fox earth, badger sett or the edge of a field or clearing where you will have a clear view.
- 'Spy-out' the place some days before and find some good places to sit comfortably.
- Come back, before sunset, on a warm, still evening.

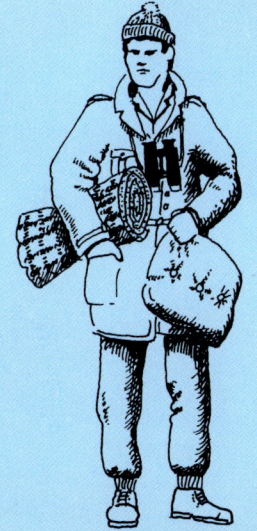

- Make sure you approach the site towards any breeze that is blowing.
- Do not walk around leaving your scent on the ground. Sit down against a tree and keep still and quiet.
- Watch in the direction from which the breeze is coming. Sit "down-wind" of the entrance to an earth or sett.
- Move only your eyes. If you must move head or arms do so only very, very slowly.
- Take a cushion, insect-repellant and clothing to keep warm and prevent insects biting your skin. An old dark blanket with a hole for your head is a good idea.

PREDATOR & PREY

The large carnivores or flesh eaters have long disappeared from Britain and most of Europe – animals such a the lynx, wolf and bear. The few small carnivorous animals and birds that are left are probably having less effect than would be the case if human influence were removed.

Most of a group of animals which include the wolverine, the badger, the martens, minks and stoats and the polecat (from which we have bred the ferret) have disappeared or exist only in remote places. The same is true of the larger birds of prey, the eagles, buzzards and harriers.

Field Vole

Woodmouse

Our own pets, the cat and dog and ferrets which often escape, are also to some extent countryside predators. Because for many centuries the only enemy of the fox or deer has been human beings, it may be that both are now present in the countryside in greater numbers than for centuries – they have no other natural enemies.

Perhaps the smallest carnivorous mammal and the most ferocious for its size is the shrew. Shrews, which are related to the mole and not to mice or voles, feed on invertebrate creatures in almost underground tunnels

Common Shrew

During past centuries mammals and birds have been persecuted by humans throughout the countryside and especially where the woods are preserved for game. The stoat and weasel, however, perhaps because they are smaller and can hide more easily, have been more successful. The larger fox, a scavenger as well as a predator, has in effect been preserved for the purpose of fox-hunting. In many places throughout the countryside small woods or fox coverts have been created to provide a home base for the fox from which he can be driven by the hunt.

beneath the litter of leaves in the bottom of hedges, copses and woods. Like the mole, they hardly need daylight and hunt by scent. They ignore the day and night pattern of life, which most animals follow, and hunt until they have found enough worms or beetles – say 30 minutes and then they sleep until hunger awakes them again in 30-45 minutes. Living at a very fast rate they need a lot of food, perhaps eating their own weight of food in 24 hours.

Although the other small mammals, mice and voles, eat an unknown amount of insect food in the summer they are really vegetarians eating seeds, fruit, berries, shoots, bark and in the case of the Field Vole mostly grass. Two of the mice, the Harvest mouse and the Common or Hazel Dormouse are scarce. The most common in woods and hedgerows are the Woodmouse and its near relative the Yellow-necked Mouse. House mice are usually found nearer human habitation. The Bank Voles keep to the hedges and copses but wherever grass grows tall and rough there live the Field Voles. Those two voles and the mice can increase in numbers very rapidly, but because they form the major

Weasel

food of so many predators the balance of numbers is usually restored quickly. Since rabbits have become less numerous due to disease, these mice and voles have featured largely in the diet of the fox. Weasels in particular hunt them on the ground and the kestrel and the owl search for them from the air. Most of these predators then are friends of the farmer – providing he keeps his chickens locked up.

VISITORS – PAST AND PRESENT

Lots of animals, birds and insects are rare now but once were common.
- A visit to your local museum's natural history section will surprise you when you discover what used to occur where you live – 50 or a 100 years ago!
- You might try to make a list and ask why each has disappeared.
- There are others brought to this country from abroad that have now escaped and live "wild". Maybe the museum can tell you about them.
- Bats are useful and interesting mammals that have become quite rare. You can help them by building a Bat-box for their use in summer time. It should be like a bird nest box but without the hole in the front. Instead there should be a gap at the back of the floor of the box as shown in the illustration. It should be sited in a large shady tree or high on a sheltered wall.

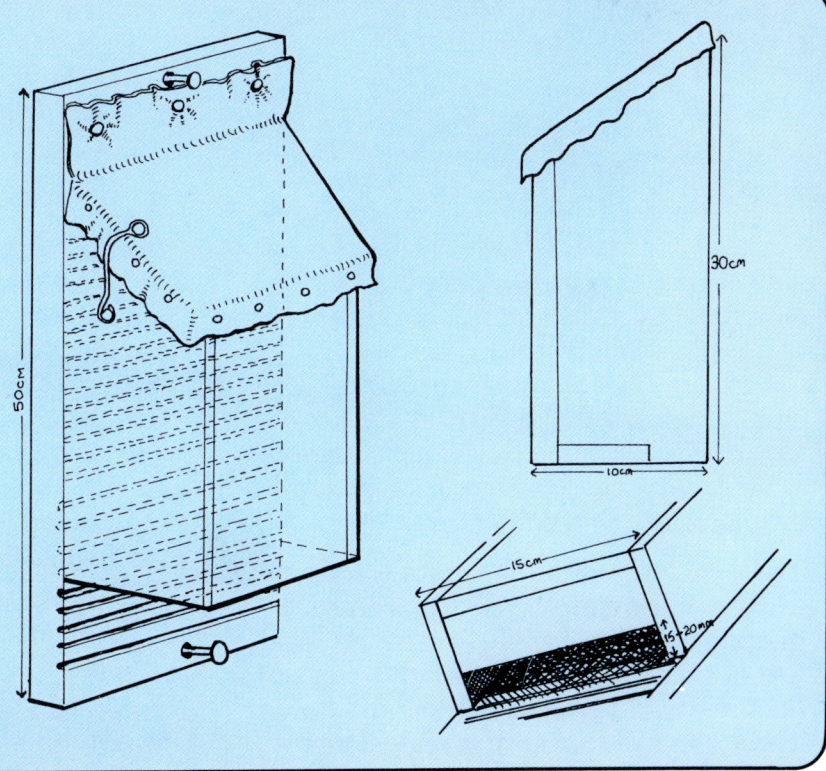

COUNTRY TRACKING

Fox hunting rabbits at dawn

The trail of an animal or bird left across snow, sand or mud is usually a record of its movement over the ground and what appears as a "set" of animal tracks was not necessarily made at the same moment of time – the forefeet will have left the snow and are on their way to make the next footprints as the larger hind feet land slightly ahead of the marks left by the forefeet.

Trails will vary with the type of creature and whether it is hopping, walking, trotting, running or galloping. The second day of snow, that is after a night when the snow lies across the fields, will show many trails and tracks. Those you will find most often will be the twin hopping trails of blackbirds and thrushes, the "pigeon-toed" trails of wood pigeons, numerous tracks left by rabbits and the stealthy, 'one-foot-at-a-time', trail of a hunting fox. If the snow is very deep most trails will form a different pattern, for instance, the fox will need to "bound" along instead of walking and the short legged squirrel will not clear the snow between tracks leaving the mark of his bushy tail in the centre.

'Trailing' in the snow will tell you many things; where the fox stopped to mark his territory, where he sat down on a slight rise in the ground – probably to sniff the air, as his trail then changed direction – and where a few

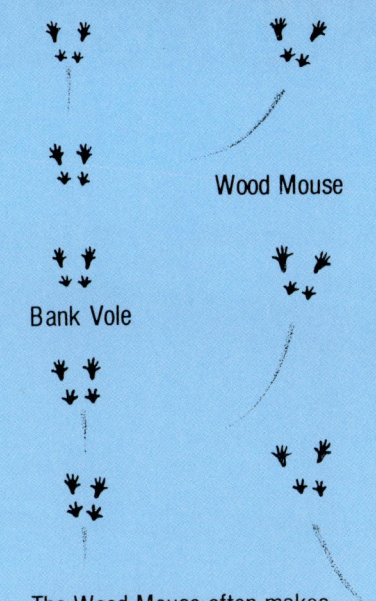
feathers tell us he delved with his nose into the bottom of the hedge and took a roosting Dunnock. The solitary trail of a pheasant picking his way along the hedge will contrast with a 'traffic jam' of tracks where a covey of partidges followed each other through a gap between grass tussocks.

You will be surprised by the amount of activity and by the distance covered by many creatures just to find tiny quantities of food. Failure to find sufficient food before dusk means, for many birds, a frozen death during the night or being too weak by morning to find food or escape from predators. The snow shows that Bullfinches frequently work the hedgerow brambles feeding on the tiny dried blackberry seeds. Only when there is snow everywhere is it possible to see how important various food sources are to different birds.

Stoat   Badger   Fox
(not to scale)

Shrew   Mouse   Hedgehog

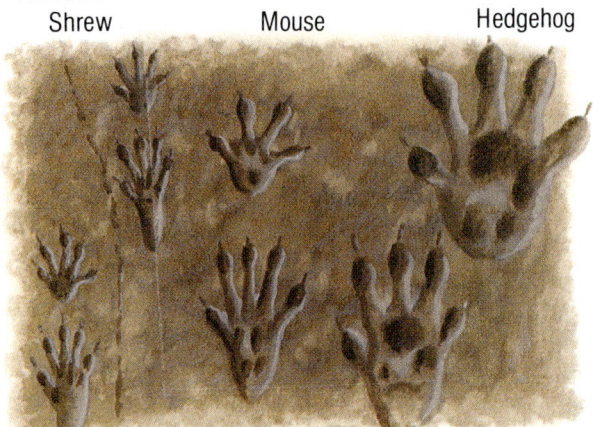

(not to scale)

Try to follow one trail to see where, and how far it goes. You may be lucky and see where a stoat chased a rabbit or a weasel carried a mouse in its mouth (the tail of the mouse marking the snow). Most frequently you will find the marks of wing feathers where a bird took off or landed.

The snow will train your eyes to see much more than you did before. Once the snow has melted away the signs of feeding and movement along the trails through hedge and ditch will still be there – but will be more difficult to see.

SIGNS & CLUES

A badger passed this way.

Sometimes clues and signs left behind are easier to see than the creatures themselves; this is certainly true of many mammals. The secret is in acquiring the skill of knowing where to look and what to look for; once you have found the evidence, the story it tells is usually only common sense.

Perhaps the easiest way to begin is not to look for tracks and then scratch your head in bewilderment, but to watch birds and animals in suitable places – such as the muddy edges of rivers and ponds – and then go to look at the tracks you saw the bird or animal make. Draw and measure them in your notebook. Watch a squirrel eating beech nuts and then examine the scraps and husks it left behind.

Follow animals with binoculars, note where they cross a ditch, go through a hedge entering or leaving a wood and where they drink at a stream. Then visit those places to record the tracks. A stream after a flood following heavy rain is a fine place to spend a few hours noting the wealth of signs in the new silt and mud. After a snowfall you learn more than at any other time about the mammals and birds in your area. Give them time to make the tracks! Wait at least 24 hours and then start exploring. Having found a well used gap in a hedge you will quickly realise that others use it too. One gap may well be used by fox, badger, rabbit and hare. Paths and tracks will appear to radiate in all directions from the gap if you start looking carefully.

Bank voles and wood mice will have tunnels and runs leading under fallen logs. Carefully turn the logs over if you can, and you will find feeding hollows surrounded by piles of empty nut shells and seed cases. Turn the log back again! There will be droppings also and these are clues as well. In the winter, especially after the snow has melted you will find bark gnawing has provided food for many creatures – often under the snow – and then the droppings of field or bank voles will tell the woodman who to blame.

However, teeth marks are usually the main evidence where trees have been gnawed. Where the teeth marks are large and there are cloven hoof prints you will know it was deer. With hares, look for the height they may reach above ground by standing on their hind legs, as well as the lines made by the ridged teeth and the pale coarse capsule-shaped droppings that may be nearby. Deer droppings are black and quite different but equally characteristic.

Starling using Woodpecker hole.

WHERE TO LOOK

On your next walk look carefully in the sort of places listed below. You can be sure to find things, you can be sure you will be surprised and you will feel rather pleased with your improved powers of observation; the countryside will never be the same again.

WHERE TO LOOK	WHAT TO EXPECT
under a log or woodpile (replace)	hibernating animals, piles of seeds, husks and food remains, droppings. Bits of insects, etc.
carefully behind loose bark (do not completely remove it)	hibernating insects, spider funnel traps, old nests, roosting sites (do not destroy, such places are important)
dead trees devoid of bark	squirrel scratchings (4 and 5 toes) insect borings, bird attacks for larvae, nest holes.
an isolated stump	a feeding platform – for squirrels? food remains, husks, etc., bird droppings, examine for seeds.
beneath a dead branch on an exposed tree or prominent fence post.	pellets of birds of prey and owls; bird droppings for the seeds and skins of fruit eaten; unusual plants growing from past seeds.
bottles in ditches, bushes, etc.	skeletons and remains of small mammals.
holes in trees.	look – just inside the edge and the ground beneath – for gnawings, greasy smudging, droppings, or mud around entrance.
holes in ground or banks.	Note:– size, smell? size of spoil heap, food remains, any tracks, hairs, scratchings nearby, droppings or 'latrines'.
holes or gaps in hedges and fences.	tracks, hair or fur caught on wire or thorns.
crossing or drinking points on streams; muddy patches on paths.	tracks (take care where your tracks go)
clear ground under trees.	for signs of feeding in the canopy above; nibbled shoots, husks of nuts and fruit or buds.
long dead grass.	tunnels and runs of voles etc. at ground or roots level.
narrow paths 2-15 cms. wide.	ground surface worn, tracks when wet leading to? or from?

Under trees in early Spring you may well find the scattered new chippings of wood that should cause you to look above to find the Woodpecker's hole. Note the spot and return to watch in May when you might see the young being fed. Neat little scrapings in the leaf mould are usually the work of rabbits and tunnels into the vegetation show you the way they usually go.

Dead trees that have lost their bark are the best places to look and learn the scratches made by squirrels. Just as the animals entering the wood will have regular pathways, so will the squirrels have pathways through the trees. Unless in panic, they never run along a branch without knowing that the end leads to another and yet another branch.

Holes in trees might be made by woodpeckers and if clean and round are still in use. If however wisps of bark bass or dried grass hang out maybe squirrels have taken over, or, if white droppings are soiling the entrance it is usually the mark of starlings. If the edge of the hole is gnawed and bitten you may be sure squirrels are in residence.

Owl pellets under thick tall holly trees or ivy-clad oaks may be a clue as to who roosts there. Various roosting sites of different birds are always betrayed by droppings. There are thousands of clues and signs in every wood, hedge and field, and little searching is required for usually they are plainly visible – by constantly looking and noting you will soon realise that you too are beginning to see things that others cannot.

THE WEB OF LIFE

In the whiteness of a snowy winter, corpses and death are very noticeable, but in other seasons violent death is as frequent if not more common.

Millions of invertebrates – insects, bugs and spiders – are killing and being killed and these killers become the prey of birds and animals which in turn may be fed to the young of still larger birds and animals.

Obviously the vegetarians must always be more numerous than the carnivores or the

Fox with young Blue tit

Blue tit and young

carnivores will die of starvation. Thus in the world of insects there are more insects that feed on plants than on other insects; there are also more rabbits and mice and voles than foxes. It is also usually true that small creatures are eaten by large ones and large ones are eaten by those that are still larger. So, we find that smaller creatures tend to reproduce themselves in greater numbers than larger animals. The relationship between an animal and those it feeds on, and the food that they in turn eat is sometimes called a "food-chain".

For instance, the Moth caterpillars feeding on the hawthorn leaves are taken by Blue tits to feed their young, but the young Blue tits may be seized by Magpies when they first leave the nest to provide food for the Magpie family. A few days later a careless young Magpie may be taken as food for the young fox cubs. In a sense the chain ends with the fox who no longer has any natural enemies – but a car may kill the young fox and the food chain then completes a circle for the corpse of the fox is eaten by the larva of the blowfly or blue-bottle; scavenging carrion beetles also join in and decay caused by bacteria eventually incorporates the body of the fox into the soil of the hedge in which the hawthorn grows.

The pattern is really more complicated, however. Many different insects eat the hawthorn and many different birds eat the insects and they may fall victims to other predators – the sparrow-hawk, crow, weasel or fox. The term "food-web" or "food pyramid" describes the relationship more accurately.

MAKING A SWEEP-NET

A "sweep-net" is an easily made, and useful piece of equipment which will help you to appreciate the vast populations of small creatures that exist everywhere.

Although you can use it to catch particular insects, it is also used to collect "at random"; that is, to sweep the net through long grass, nettles and other vegetation, entrapping whatever happens to be there. If the net is kept moving constantly and then turned so that the end of the net bag hangs over the rim (as shown in illustration) all the creatures are caught in the bottom and those you wish to examine can be removed singly in specimen tubes. Beware of brambles and wild rose thorns tearing your net.

- You need wire from a clothes hanger, a short piece of broom handle and about a square metre of netting of the type used for net-curtaining.
- One edge of the netting should be hemmed to take the wire as shown in a)
- Now fold the material in half and cut as b)
- What is called a "french seam" c) is the best way to avoid the inside stiching fraying. First stitch the edges together and then turn the net inside-out before making a second row of stitching.
- Cut the clothes hanger and bend it to shape d)
- Drill a hole in the handle to take the ends of the wire e)
- Secure the net, when threaded onto the wire, to the handle as shown f)

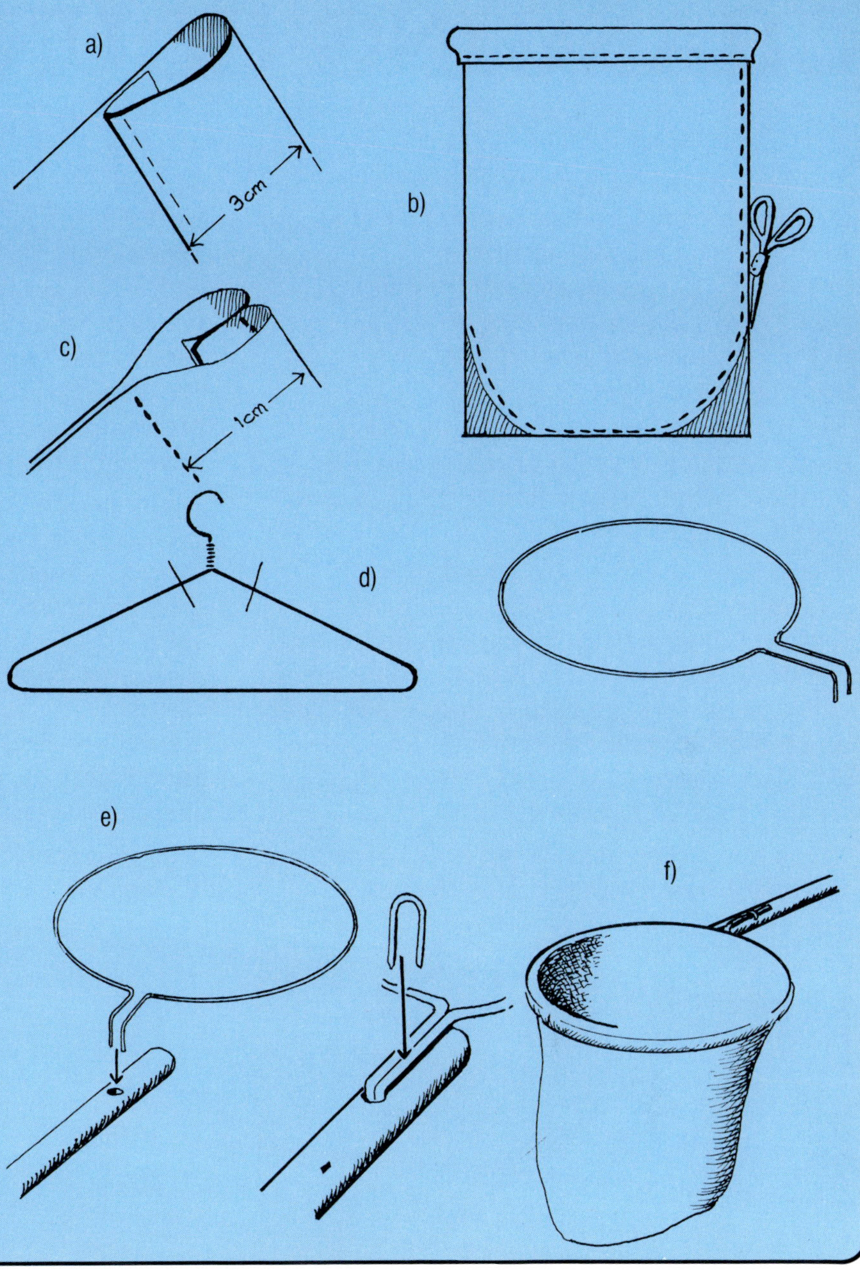

a)

3cm

b)

c)

1cm

d)

e)

f)

Work of a Leaf-cutter Bee

It is possible to start at any point, with any creature and work up or down the pattern of "what feeds on what" – try it! Always at the bottom are plants.

An increase in numbers of one insect provides others with the opportunity of plentiful food but cold weather, for the young of insect-eating birds, can be disastrous. A change in one part of the food-web affects other parts; the "balance" of life is changed. Weather can obviously cause changes, and so can humans – by cutting down a wood or removing a hedge; by replanting a wood or ploughing a field; by draining a swamp or spraying weed-killer.

Drastic changes on a large scale can cause serious disturbance, the effects of which are sometimes not noticed at first.

CHANGING COUNTRYSIDE

The countryside is important to everyone; to the farmers who produce nearly half of all our food and who use 80% of Britain's land in growing it, to all who enjoy it by walking, riding or driving or picnicing or camping, and, to our children and grandchildren who will also want to enjoy it.

But the countryside is changing – and it must change if we wish to grow more food for more people who will have more time to visit it.

The farmer wishes to grow food more efficiently. To do so he uses more machinery that need bigger fields to work in; hedges and woods are in the way. Poisonous 'weed-killers' called herbicides are used to keep fields 'clean and tidy'. Poisonous insecticides are used to kill insect pests.

At first a lot of damage was caused by over use of dangerous poisons but now farmers are learning to use more carefully the less dangerous kinds. The trouble is that herbicides if sprayed indiscriminately kill plants other than those growing in the crops and, when sprayed elsewhere, such as the banks of waterways and roadside verges just to control the "weeds", are not only depriving the countryside of the wild flowers and butterflies and other harmless insects that depend on them, but useful insects as well.

Many insects, besides bees, pollinate flowers including crops and thus are vital to the farmer. Others are important because they help to control pests. The pest insects breed more rapidly than their enemies among the predatory insects and thus when both are destroyed by the poisonous insecticide spray, the pest returns first and in greater numbers than before as it now has no enemies. More insecticide is then needed.

The pest insects, because they reproduce themselves rapidly can also develop immunity

- Ask your parents and grandparents about the changes they have noticed: were there more wild flowers, birds and butterflies when they were children than there are now?
- You can help – by reporting any large numbers of deaths, either birds or pollinating insects such as bees to your district Environmental Health Officer and perhaps your local or County Naturalists Trust.
- Try persuading people to leave nettles growing in small unused corners, not only are they good places for you to look for lots of interesting insects but some of our most colourful butterflies breed on them.
- Lastly it is important to know and persuade others to follow the **COUNTRY CODE**.

THE COUNTRY CODE is a reminder and guide for the visitor to the countryside on how to behave properly.
- Guard against all risks of fire – see that no one, including parents, throw away cigarette ends and are careful with matches.
- Fasten all gates: animals will wander causing damage and danger.
- Keep dogs under control: especially when livestock are about.
- Keep to foot paths: remember grass

is a crop too.
- Protect wild life and plants: watch, do not collect or uproot, – take only photographs.
- Take care on country roads: they are especially dangerous with bends and slow traffic or animals. Walk on the right hand side.
- Respect the life of the countryside and the ways of the people who live or work in it. Set a good example so that you or others may be welcomed again.
- Avoid damage to fences, hedges and walls: they are expensive to repair and animals can escape.
- Leave no litter: not only is it unsightly, but dangerous to livestock – especially plastic bags.
- Do not pollute water supplies in any way, or interfere with animal drinking troughs.

to the poisons quickly.

The destruction of hedges, and bushy corners of unused land also means that insect eating birds and mammals lose their breeding sites even if they are not poisoned by eating the insects. The burning of straw, after the harvest also leads to the accidental loss of trees and hedges.

The "balance-of-life" in the countryside is thus very easily disturbed and it is very difficult to make the changes that must be made without causing too many losses.

Needs

Organisations

CLOTHING:– Windproof clothing over a warm garment is usually the wisest way to dress. Dull coloured clothes which enable you to merge with your surroundings and which do not rustle will help you see more!

A NOTE-BOOK or clip-board with a waterproof plastic cover and at least 2 sharp pencils with which to record events by notes and sketches as soon as possible after they happen.

CONTAINERS:– Plastic bags, tubes, small boxes and tins. Do not forget to label them:– date, where found, etc. (your local chemist may have surplus empty containers).

A FOLDING LENS (x 8 or x 10) is a most useful piece of equipment. It is important to hold the lens between thumb and forefinger while resting the hand against your cheek. With the lens close to your eye, you should bring the specimen you are examining towards the lens until it appears in focus.

BINOCULARS:–

a) Before buying seek advice. The very cheapest is not always a wise purchase. Try several makes before deciding.

b) Consider the weight and the ease of handling. Look for brightness and clear vision. Check definition at the edges not only in the centre.

c) Binoculars marked 8 x 30: the 8 indicates the amount of magnification and 30 the size of the field of view (actually 30 mm. is the size of the larger lens).

d) 8 x 40 is a popular size. 10 x 50 might be too heavy hanging around your neck all day. Less than 7 x will not be powerful enough.

e) The R.S.P.B. have a free leaflet of advice on choosing binoculars (send a S.A.E. to:– The Lodge, Sandy, Beds. SG19 2DL).

MAPS:– Ordnance Survey maps of various scales are detailed and useful. As they are rather expensive, check in your local library which scale and sheet number will be most useful to you. Then purchase or order from a large book shop.

BIRD TABLES AND NESTBOXES:– can be obtained from the R.S.P.B. (address above); they also supply leaflets of advice should you wish to build your own.

Several organisations have youth sections, or local groups for young persons where lectures and field trips are arranged and where help and practical advice is available together with a chance to meet others with similar interests.

In many areas there is often a group of the WATCH club which is usually the junior section of the local county NATURE CONSERVATION TRUST. The County Trusts are sponsored by the Royal Society for the Promotion of Nature Conservation (R.S.P.N.C.).

Membership of WATCH will give you the chance to be involved in a wide variety of interests and activities concerned with wildlife and nature conservation. The Club's magazine "WATCHWORD" is published three times a year. For details write to "Watch", 22, The Green, Nettleham, Lincoln, LN2 2NR.

The Young Ornithologists Club (Y.O.C.) is for young people interested in bird-watching and is the junior section of the Royal Society for the Protection of Birds (R.S.P.B.). Membership entitles you to a copy of BIRDLIFE every two months and entry to R.S.P.B. reserves free or at a reduced rate.

The Council for Environmental Conservation (COENCO) have a number of small leaflets providing useful information which are free if you send a stamped and addressed envelope. They can also provide a list of your local Natural History Societies, however try your local library first.
Address: CoEnCo, Zoological Gardens, Regent's Park, London, NW1 4RY.

The World Wildlife Association is active in the conservation of wildlife in the United Kingdom but is also involved on a worldwide scale. Young people who are interested should contact the U.K. Education Section, World Wildlife Association, Panda House, 29, Grenville Street, London, EC1N 8AX.

INDEX

PRINTED IN BELGIUM BY

proost
INTERNATIONAL BOOK PRODUCTION